SELFLESS   RULERS

Table of contents

DEDICATION..

 DISCRIPTION ....

 CAST.....................

DEDICATION

to all persons of incorruptible minds and reader who bought the book

THE DISCRIPTION

*The play portrays the absurd socio-political and economic situation   in
developing countries of the world especially   in Africa. It does not.
How ever, refer to any country   in particular.*

CAST

Hon. Felix : the head of political administration
Chief Ben : an adviser to Hon. Felix
Chief Chris : A minister under Hon. Felix
Upland youth
Lowland youth
Mummy prince
Daddy prince
Mr. Bright : A citizen and a farmer
Mr. Greg :A farmer and friend of Mr. Bright
Madam Joyce : owner of restaurant
1" Expatriate
2" Expatriate

- *Hon. Philip : the new elected of political administration.*

Chief Don : A minister under Hon. Philip

Chief Richard : An adviser to Hon. Philip

CHAPTER ONE

CHORUS : *it was a land of abundance and peace reigned.*
 They where crops to be cultivated : palm. Cocoa. Rubber
Groundnut. Rice and soil was good for cultivation. The river
 A where filled with aquatic lives: fish. Lobster. Shrimp and
 They was no hunger: they were plenty to eat and plenty
 to drink.. It was a land of milk and honey...

ACT 1. SCENE 1

(it is onshore: a river in the background and boats are berth at the brink
a typical fishing community. A lady come on stage carrying her catch
of daily catch of the day's fishing a basket filled with fish. Crabs
and lobster : her husband meets her)

DADDY PRINCE :   mummy prince, you returned early. How was today's catch?

MUMMY PRINCE : daddy prince, the catch was good; you can see my
basket filled with a large quantity of fish! I pulled in fish with every

throw of the net. I've not even gone for my basket is filled with fish
. The river is practically brimming with aquatic lives.

DADDY PRINCE : the catch will bring us a good sum, with the demand for
fish's on the increase..... And I having been promoted in the company to
the position of chief security officer!

MUMMY PRINCE : promoted? You don't mean it! Why didn't you tell me?

DADDY PRINCE : now I've told you anyway I wanted to keep it until bed time
but I couldn't keep it to myself   any longer when you carried in that basket
of fish and the radiance on your face!

MUMMY PRINCE : yes, when I carried the fish to the market, the people from
upland will pay good money for them

G

DADDY PRINCE ; yes, God is certainly answering our prayers; we'll not go
hungry. We'll be able to pay the children's school fees and still have enough
put by for a rainy day. Come honey. Let me help you and sort them out

MUMMY PRINCE :   you're a darling, what would I have done without you?

DADDY PRINCE : you're the one who's the God sent. (He gives her a peck on
the cheek and together, the carry the basket of fish inside.)

LIGHT FADE OUT.

ACT 1, SCENE ii

(Mr. Bright and Mr. Greg are in a restaurant owned by madam Joyce.
they are In a round table with bottles of chilled beer on the table
. They are facing each other, drinking their beer while chatting.)

Mr. Bright: (He raises his glass which is half- filled with beer, sips the beer and drops the glass on the table) How is your family, Mr. Greg?

Mr. Greg: thank God, we're fine. The harvest was beautiful and my rubber trees are doing well... Since the rubber manufacturing company came to the land business has progress. We're not complaining

Mr. Bright: how right you are! The coming of the expatriate to the land has improved the economy and commerce is simply booming. I now export palm oil since my production has increased due the processing machine that I installed last year. Business have risen

Mr. Greg; (pouring beer from the bottles into his glass.) God is simply wonderful

Mr. Bright:(noticing that the bottle is empty) shall we have another bottle of beer?

Mr. Greg: of course.... You're generous.

Mr. Bright: (raising his voice to call the bar owner) madam Joyce !

Madam Joyce: yes! (she comes and stands before them)

Mr. Bright: bring us two more bottles and they should be chill

Madam Joyce : yes sir. (going in to bring the drinks, and the pause as an afterthought and says.) there's pizza and chicken.

Mr. Bright: (stares at Mr. Greg as if to pass on massage: Mr. Greg nods, almost imperceptibly) okay, bring two chicken and two pizza

Mr. Greg: are you aware my son is getting married in the next four months time

Mr. Bright: how could I? Am just hearing that for the first time, I wasn't aware

Mr. Greg : the invitation will soon be out he's is marrying in London

Mr. Bright: London? Do you know my wife is also from London?

Mr. Greg: O-yes, I'm aware. But the bride prince of the London woman's is very high

Mr. Bright: Ha. Ha ha.... But they made good housewife

Mr. Greg: I don't think the London bride price will be too much for us to pay anyway, since business is booming

LIGHT FADE OUT.

ACT1; SCENE iii

(two friends in the their mid-twenties are strolling and talking along

a major street in the land. In excitement, they recounted
the experience of their just concluded one-year national youth service)

Lowland youth: how was your youth service year?

Upland youth: it was wonderful. I served in the west. I enjoyed
every bit of it My Orientation   must of all. To be free from stress
of school life! The orientation camp was really interesting

Lowland youth: I served in the East... As you already said; the Camp was truly
exciting. But what I found irking where the early morning and afternoon drills

Upland youth: yes.... That too was part of the excitement. You are right,
at the end I felt like a veteran soldier

Lowland youth: what excited me the most was the people over there..
to see so many youth of different backgrounds gathered together, Living
together, playing together, sharing the same experience like one big family.

Upland youth: yes, yes...... And after that, the college assignment. I was
posted to a college for college assignments..

Lowland youth:(Interrupting Upland Youth) I too, at first I was scared
to teach.

Upland youth: I was not scared one bit. In fact, I was thrilled to be really
teaching.

Lowland youth: though when I saw that the students where cooperative,
I began to enjoy teaching. Besides, most of my students were eager to lean

Upland youth : in my own case, the students were really cooperative and
the hospital are generous

Lowland youth: cold you believe that the town where I served the
bosses there use to give us pizza and gizzard every day?

Upland youth: ours was also same as you guys

Lowland youth: (think) that remind me, what your plan now you
are done with college

Upland youth: well I will further my education not yet. I have about three
chance to work right now. Mr. Greg, who is into rubber processing, want
to go into rubber fabrics and he asked me to manage it, there's is also a
vacancy for the position of mechanical engineer in a construction   company
that I know of besides, my plan to be self employed you are aware that I
read mechanical engineering, and I've succeeded convincing an uncle
of mine to sponsor a hard where manufacturing firm which I will manage

Lowland youth: that we be wonderful.

Upland youth: it will pay off; I know it will, with lot of hard work, of course . But once we get our footing, it'll be smooth sailing. What're your plan?

Lowland youth: just like you.... I've got several chances, but I have not really made up my mind, a leading bank in town need graduate as cashier. There's also this multinational company that has vacancies for the position of accountant. But the one that appeal to me most is the state house that is presently employing graduates to fill in vacant positions.

Upland youth: I think the state house is more appealing.

Lowland youth ; that also what I thought, but the salary...

Upland youth: (Interrupting Lowland youth) it should not be about money, Job security should also be considered.

Lowland youth: of course, I know that

Upland youth: as for me, my mind is set on being self-employed.

Lowland youth: how are your parents? I'll be coming over for a visit ; I really enjoyed that meal I ate at your place the last time I came visiting.

Upland youth: Ha. Ha. ha... Thank you. My parents are fine and they extend their greetings.

Lowland youth: how about your younger sister, Lucy. She should be in her second year at the university now..

Upland youth: yes. in her second year..... They should be rounding off the second semester exam if I'm not mistaken. That reminds me! Your annual cultural festival comes up next month. It is a festival I cannot afford to miss. Just to watch those maiden dancers from different places is a joy to behold

Lowland youth: but I think yours better - that combat and karate dance. And music every where it is a show of Manliness, a show of bravery.

Upland youth: ours is too rowdy and violent; a mere believe of long fault battle. Festivals should be thing of pleasure.... With fanfare and dance. Do you know that the American girl girls are the best in the festival

Lowland youth: that rather primitive.

Upland youth: well.... It been nice seeing you again after such a long time.

Lowland youth: it's been really nice.... I hope to see you soon

Upland youth: take of yourself body...

Lowland youth: you too body..

LIGHT FADE OUT

CHAPTER TWO

ACT ii SCENE 1

*(it in Hon. Felix's palace, he sits on his house and before him are the
minister, chief Chris and 1" expatriate)*

Hon. Felix : so it true you have discovered large quantity of
minerals in our land?

1" expatriate : yes, your lordship the land is blessed to have this type
of rare mineral, and when dug the refined, much wealth will come to
the land, riches beyond our imagination and land Will be elevated to
those of Europe, America and other developed countries of the world..

Hon. Felix (Laughing and very happy.) Ha. ha ha(and turning to Chief Chris,
he asks.) dis you hear that? Didn't you head the good news?

Chief Chris: it is indeed good news, your lordship.

Hon. Felix: (turning again to 1" Expatriate.) how soon can we....
Em .... Dig out mineral?

1" **Expatriate**: your lordship, I should say within the year. We
will first get equipment to enable us excavate to the dep't where
the mineral is, and then we will bring it to the surface.

Hon. Felix: Yes. Yes

1" **Expatriate**: yes, your lordship, we will bring the minerals to the
surface, we refine and then we sell

Hon. Felix : I am very happy for this piece of good news yes,
very happy. I'll give approval for the excavation , for digging. But
first see the minister, chief Chris, tomorrow morning for proper briefing.

1" **Expatriate** : yes, your lordship (1" Expatriate take his leave.)

Hon. Felix : (turning to face chief Chris) you hard what he said?

Chief Chris : yes, your lordship

Hon. Felix: the land will soon be transformed into great wealth
beyond our imagination. Those were his very worlds : our land ; my
land and your land like ancient. Egypt, Rome.(He look at chief Chris
and smile) we Will be great and powerful.... (He stand facing chief
Chris, looking at him eyeballs to eyeballs. In all seriousness he says)
we shall take advantage of the situation to enrich ourselves

Chief Chris: yes, your lordship

Hon. Felix : you're going to establish a contracting firm known as
chop contracting company or CCC. You be CEO as my subordinate,
of course, and in any government contract, the CCC. Shall be given

to priority to handle it. The process will be shared among us, the CCC executive.

Chief Chris: (Nodding his head in agreement.) yes, your lordship, sir.

LIGHT FADE OUT

ACT ii, SCENE ii

(it is the following morning : 1" and 2" Expatriate are in chief Chris office briefing, and collection of latter approval for the excavation of the ground and the extraction of the mineral. It a big office. Chief Chris is site behind a big table, facing the two Expatriates.)

Chief Chris : (he clear his throat and begins.) you're very much welcome.(He pause and continues after some seconds) his lordship Hon. Felix has ask me to give you go ahead for the excavation of the ground for this rich minerals as soon as possible . But must understand this. That we'll undertake the contract . You'll contact the manager of chop contracting company for further details

1" **Expatriate** : honorable minister, sir, I mean no disrespect, but for

this work of exciting, we need technicians, experts and not just anybody?
Chief Chris: is it not digging? What so special about digging?

2" **Expatriate**: chief, what we are saying is that, it's not just digging. . I mean the ordinary digging with spade and shovels. We need special machines will create in roads into the ground to enable men go in to

shift this mineral out I. In doing this we need a body of expert. And
we don't know, chief, if the CCC is capable of producing such expert...

Chief Chris: (frowning.) I don't know what you're talking about.... Expert...
Technicians..... I say the contract has been awarded to the CCC.

1"Expatriate: I beg your pardon sir. But, sir can we employ our own
body of experts, to work with us? I am sorry to say sir, that without
their technical know-how, it would be impossible to understand this work

2" Expatriate : honorable minster. Sir. What my colleague is saying
is that the CCC can provide laborer's, while we employ our own staff.

Chief Chris: (holding up his hand as a signal for 2" Expatriate to stop.)
that is Exactly what I'm saying. You bring your own body of expertise
and technician and CCC provides the manpower. But they are rules I.

1" Expatriate: Rules?

Chief Chris: Not rules anyway, but conditions that are attached to the
contract. Besides, it is an affordable task. (He pause and continue again). Well,
the condition is that you are to give me thirty percent of whatever paid to you.

1" Expatriate: (showed amazement) sir...

Chief Chris: (holding up his hand.) that's how we operate here. I'm the middle man and without me the contract will not be given to you. I will talk to his lordship, Hon. Felix to award you this contract. Yes. I will convince him that you people are capable of doing the job. As the middle man or agent ; call it whatever name you choose, my fee is thirty percent. (the two Expatriate exchange bewildered glances.)

Chief Chris:(Open his draw and brings out a sheet of paper.) here is the agreement. If you agreed to mine condition all you have to do is to sign and the contract is surly yours.

1" Expatriate:(clear throat.) honorable minister, sir. When we start excavating, there will be some sort of population to the immediate environment; the rivers, the surrounding forest and there's people ; the host community has to be compensated adequately

Chief Chris : I've told you the terms; we shall settle the host communities
. If you want the contract, just sign

2" Expatriate: honorable minister, sir. Can we get to you first thing tomorrow morning?

Chief Chris: I'll give you twenty for hours if I don't hear from you, the contract goes to another firm. I believe you me clearly or should I repeat myself?

Two Expatriate: yes, sir. (they hastily pack their documents into their briefcase.
They walk towards the door as chief Chris signals them to leave)

LIGHT FADE OUT

ACT ii, SCENE iii

*(light opened in Hon. Felix's palace. The palace is expensively furnished.
Present are , chief Ben and chief Chris. Hon. Felix sits comfortably
on his throne with his two subordinate in a meeting)*

Hon. Felix : thank you gentlemen for responding to my summons at such
short notice. I'll not waste your time but will go straight to the matter
at hand. (He pause for a while before he continued). It Is this year budget
. The money we're going to approve for this year's budget is going to be much
than last year's own, because this year's expenditure is going to be big, I mean
very much big.

Chief Ben: your lordship, the fact remains that we, did a lot for people
last year and yet they still complained. And they was a lot of criticism
from some quarters especially the opposition.

Hon. Felix :that's where our mistakes lies. We pampered our
subjects too much, a lot and they became lazy, spoiled, disloyal
. They had room to maneuver and this has led to the criticism
. Now we shall herd then as a shepherd herds his sheep, make them obey
without questioning and look without seeing..... We shall make them toe
the line

Chief Ben: your lordship... How do we achieve this?

Hon. Felix : that a very good question. Firstly we began by hardworking the populace. We announced the amount of the is year's budget, but shall only use about one quarter while we share the remaining three quarter , while we share the remaining three quarters amongst the ruling class . All contract shall be awarded to us, the elite..... Yes, the executives . And any contract awarded to an independent contractor ; such contractor must remit thirty percent of the gross profits to us we shall pay the working class peanut as salaries and the ruling class would be paid fortunes. This way we'll put fear in the minds of the people and they will tremble before us and no one will dare oppose us. ..

Chief Chris; you're right, your lordship. When I made our position known to the Expatriate handling the mineral project, they consented and readily signed the agreement.

Chief Ben: in that case. Your lordship, I will advise that. With his lordship approval, the CCC should spread and have branches in all the states with our headquarters here .in the land. In this respect we'll have our hand in all government projects.

Hon. Felix :(He turned to the minister) chief Chris, see to that the CCC have branches in all the states and that the CCC has a hand in all government projects; such as electricity, roads, housing, etc. all that maximum cost. The cost of executing any project should be inflated to the highest

Chief Chris: yes your lordship.

LIGHT FADE OUT

ACT ii, SCENE iv

*(mummy and daddy prince are alone in their living room; a room with
no furniture, except a mat in a corner, a bucket and spoons and few plates
. They both wear mourning faces as if they had been weeping.)*

Mummy prince: the company has rendered us bankrupt yes, bankrupt.
The river have been polluted and all the fish's inside are dead
... Our only hope of livelihood and survival snatched away from us

Daddy prince : what about the compensation they promised
us they will pay?

Mummy prince: what compensation? I asked what compensation
are you talking about?(She lamented; dabbing at her eyes with dirty
clothes she is putting on) we went to meet the government, the
government told us that it is the contracting firm that suppose to pay
us the compensation. We went to the contracting firm and they referred
us back to the government. We were simply pushed from pillar to post.

Daddy prince: and we are really hungry, starvation is staring us in the face
. Now that the company in which I was the chief security has folded up
because of the power outrage in the land things are really difficult
. I would have been rendering my services to those bricklayers as
a helper, But age is no longer on my side, I get ties easily these days.

Mummy prince : the government is wicked; all those so called
executives are wicked and insensitive to the suffering of populace

*(Light fade out, grows very dim and expanded again, and pick up
Mr. Bright, and Mr. Greg in madam Joyce's restaurant as usual
. The hardship and suffering of the populace, and the decayed
infrastructure in the land is the topic.)*

Mr. Greg: My rubber trees are nearly dead and the latex from the
few surviving ones is not enough even to fill a can. It has to do with
chemical from the mineral excavation site.

Mr. Bright : we're in the same boat ;my palm oil processing marching
practically useless with out electricity.

Mr. Greg : power outraged in the land is becoming a major problem
. Can you believe for the past one year my street has being without electricity?

Mr. Bright: one year? Don't make me laugh mine street has being
without electricity for the past three years. There are street that has
being in blackout for about four, five, six years..... We're already used
to the constant blackout.

Mr. Greg : this power outrage has brought a lot of hardship in
the land. Many companies have relocated to other states; firm
have short down because they can not operate   on the high cost
of the petrol and diesel

Mr. Bright: you're talking of companies and firms. What about the
artisans, those little self employed business that abounds in the

land? Saloons, cold-rooms, Weirder, tailor, you just name it how
can they run business on generators, with the high cost of petrol?
(Raising his voice to attract attention of the bar attendant, he called out.)
madam Joyce.

Madam Joyce : sire!

Mr. Bright: please bring us more beer and pizza with some meat..
We know the drinks are not cold, so please don't repeat yourself..
 (Mr. Bright and Mr. Greg laugh)

Madame Joyce: it's not our fault. We have been with out electricity
for ten months now. Five months earlier the electric power people
came and installed a new transformer and took away the faulty one
that was installed only worked for few months and them it exploded,
almost setting the whole area on fire. And we have remained in the
blackout.

Mr. Greg : where is the land heading to? No electricity, no road, no Job,
nothing at all.......

Mr. Bright (Interrupting Mr. Greg.) talking of roads, I don't even know
the one that's worse, the road or the power outage. The road in the
land are very bad that a journey of three hour's Will take you a full day..

Mr. Greg: and what is the cause of all these? Is it not corruption?
Many of our leaders are so corrupt and they think of nothing
else other Than to add to their ill-gotten wealth.

Mr. Bright: last year two of our leaders where jailed in Europe
for money laundering. The name of our land is synonymous

with corruption and anyone that claim to come from this land
is Automatically seen as a criminal or fraudster.

Mr. Greg : we should pray for credible leaders who'll redeem
the situation

Mr. Bright: yes. Yes

LIGHT FADE OUT

*(grows very dim and expands again and pick up lowland and
upland youths conversing together in a sparsely furnished one
room apartment; both are sitting on a mattress placed on the
floor; a center table and some books on top made up furniture)*

Lowland youth: are you aware that the multinational   company
where I work is preparing relocation to our neighboring country
because of the epileptic power supply   in the land?

Upland youth: my plight Is even worse. Our hardware manufacturing
firm has shutdown production for the past one year because of the
cost of buying fuel to run our generators in this area of power outrage.

Lowland youth: that's bad.... Very. very bad. What should I do when
this company leaves ? Start afresh? Start looking for work all over again?

Upland youth: no doubt about it, we're facing hectic times.

Lowland youth : it has now come to an extent that our money is valueless. The citizens prefer using the more valued foreign currency in the land instead of our own.

Upland youth: why should they deal on currency? When they know that a briefcase of foreign currency is more valuable than a houseful of the land and money.

Lowland youth: I say again where do I start from, with employment so scarce in this hard time.

Upland youth: if you don't have a God father or a politician who'll lobby for you then forget it.

Lowland youth: how do we survive then. On empty stomachs?

Upland youth: the only survival means for youth in this our land today is to be an taxi rider that If you can be able to afford one.

Lowland youth: but how can you imagine a graduate, to condescend so low as to become an taxi driver? It's does not make sense.

Upland youth: in the absence of industries, companies, roads, electricity, do the best you can do for your self, you can be self employed

Lowland youth: may God help our land........

      CHAPTER THREE

          ACT THREE

ACT III, SCENE I

(This scene is at Hon. Felix's palace: as usual, on his throne, With him are the minister, Chris and Chief Ben, the adviser to Hon. Felix .)

Hon Felix: How is the project going? (He directs the question at the minister.)

Chief Chris: Your Lordship, Sir. I brought the contractor who is in charge of all contracts awarded to CCC so that his Lordship can hear from him.

Hon. Felix: (Staring a Contractor and nodding his head as indication for Contractor to speak up.) Yes?

Contractor: Your Lordship, Sir. I am sorry to say, Sir, that the funds made available will not cover the projects.

Hon. Felix: (Addressing the minister.) Didn't you tell him about our plans?

Chief Chris: | did, Your Lordship.

Contractor: Your Lordship, Sir, the honorable minister did mentioned something about sub-standard materials

Hon. Felix: Yes, use sub-standard materials, so as to save cost. In that case we would have enough for ourselves.

Contractor : I fully agree with His Lordship, but (He looks at Hon, Felix to read his mood before he continue.) Permission to address something here, Your Lordship.

Hon. Felix :Yes, go on?

Contractor : Your Lordship, Sir. I am in total agreement to use sub-standard materials. But as for the bridge project, using sub-standard materials can lead to its collapse in the near future. The damage it will cost to lives and properties will be so much. If His Lordship will agree with me, I will suggest standard materials for the bridge project. Your Lordship.

Chief Chris : What about the transformers and the roads?
Contractor: Honorable Minister, Sir. We can import refurbished transformers at very low cost and the construction of the roads will be three inches thick instead of six, We can even make it two inches.

Hon. Felix. And you still say the money is not enough?

Contractor : Yes, Sir, Your Lordship.

Hon. Felix : Then we will! Not complete the bridge. It can be half
completed, one-third completed, do it according to the funds available

. This is our last tenure in office. The incoming administration will complete
it. How do you imagine we bought houses abroad and enjoy such
enormous wealth? By being squeamish?

Contractor : No, Your Lordship.

Chief Chris : When the transformers starts generating faults or
do not produce lights, and the roads start cracking up,
the in-coming administration 'will continue from there.

Hon. Felix : As it is we have done enough for & the populace, I
think gentlemen the meeting is over.

Chief Chris And **contractor** (together) yes your lordship

LIGHT FADE OUT

ACT III, SCENE ii

(*On a street in the land: Upland and Lowland Youths are locked
in hot exchange of words, throwing blames at each other. Lt
degenerated into a fight. They fight and inflict injuries on each
other. Mr. Bright and Mr. Greg come and separate them. The
youths go different ways with bloodied limbs and torn clothes
. Mr. Bright and Mr. Greg are left together and they talk about
what happening in the land.*)

Lowland Youth: (Shouting.) It is because Hon. Felix, that corrupt leader,

is from your area, that is why he has concentrating in developing The
Upland 'areas only.

Upland youth: (Getting angry.) You don't know what you're talking
about. We all know that Hon. Felix is related to both sides. His father
is from the Upland and his mother a lowland person.

Lowland youth : That's why he has neglected the Lowland.

Upland youth: We all know that this administration has done nothing
for the land … we know that this administration is corrupt. Lowland youth
: Hon. Felix is the head; his administration has brought this hardship
on the people and he's from the Upland.

Upland youth: What about the minister for power and energy?
Is he not from the lowland? Has he not -° succeeded in making
us live in perpetual blackouts?

Lowland youth :What about the minister that was caught and jailed for money laundering abroad? Is he not from the upland?

Upland Youth: Several Lowland ministers have also been accused of embezzlement of public funds

Lowland youth :I say it again ... and will continue to say it. There's more development in the Upland than in the Lowland! Upland youth : and I say Lowland people are discriminatory and sentimental.

Lowland Youth: (Shouting with agitation.) it is the Upland people that have brought the suffering in the land! Pompous people!

Upland Youth: it is the Lowland people that brought corruption to the land! The land was free of corruption, but the of corruption, but the Lowland people came with their cunning, hideous minds...

Lowland Youth: 'You lie! You Upland people are very good liars, good at propaganda , that's what you people are known for

Upland youth : the People of the Lowland have bitten more than they can chew. We'll soon come for you!
Lowland youth : I'm a Lowland youth ,..just Wait and I'll tell you that I'm a lowland youth! (They clash : exchanging blows and kicks. Mr. Bright and Mr. Greg rush in and separate them. Lowland and Upland Youths went their different ways to nurse their wounds.)

Mr. Bright : Did you see what corruption. has caused in the land?

Mr. Greg : This is our land where people of different tribes live in harmony a land of milk and honey; but greed has turned it to a land of violence.

Mr. Bright : The people are hungry, angry and frustrated due to the economic stagnation and in their frustration, they hit at one another.

Mr. Greg : The other day a group of Lowland youths were singing slogans, blaming the hardship in the land on the Upland people.

Mr. Bright : yesterday some sets of Upland youth armed with fuel set a Lowland man's house on fire! And the policemen on patrol did not raise eyebrows.

Mr. Greg: I think we should go inside. It is no longer safe to remain outdoors at night in the land .

Mr. Bright: O yes, we should do that!

ACT III, SCENE III

(daddy and mummy prince are together in the house, afraid to venture out as the violence and hunger in the land persists).

Mummy prince : Daddy prince, going to the market these days
is dangerous. Those of us from the Lowland are terrorized by
the Upland youths, because the market is Situated in the Upland area.

To be continued